An  EdTechTeam Collaboration

The Google Cardboard BOOK

EXPLORE, ENGAGE, AND EDUCATE WITH VIRTUAL REALITY

Holly Clark, Sylvia Duckworth,
Jeffery Heil, David Hotler,
Donnie Piercey, and Lisa Thumann

The Google Cardboard Book

© 2017 by EdTechTeam

These books are available at special discounts when purchased in quantity for use as premiums, promotions, fundraising and educational use. For inquiries and details, contact the publisher: edtechteam.com/press.

Published by EdTechTeam Press

Library of Congress Control Number: 2016956936
Paperback ISBN: 978-1-945167-19-5
eBook ISBN: 978-1-945167-20-1

Irvine, California

CONTENTS

Top 10 Reasons to Use Virtual Reality in the Classroom

By @MariaGalanis & @Andrea_Trudeau

1. Travel to and explore places all over the world without leaving the classroom

2. Develop empathy for communities in crisis by stepping into their shoes

3. Experience different careers first-hand

4. Explore the depths of the ocean and the vastness of space

5. Time travel to key events and places from the past

I have a dream...

6. Explore within the human body

7. Allow students to share their world with others by creating their own VR content

8. Discover how VR can be used in other industries like medicine, engineering, entertainment and real estate

9. Explore how VR can be integrated into every subject area and curriculum

MATH SOCIAL STUDIES PHYS ED SCIENCE LANGUAGE ARTS MUSIC DRAMA VISUAL ARTS

10. Promote curiosity and wonder!

@sylviaduckworth

Chapter 1
What is Google Cardboard?

David Hotler

As a child, I spent many hours gazing into my View-Master® Stereoscope. Image after image filled me with feelings of excitement and wonder at being immersed in a different world. With each swish of the lever, new scenes rotated into focus. No other toy succeeded in removing me so completely from my current reality. Like the stereoscopic viewers of our childhood, Google Cardboard and other virtual reality (VR) viewers serve a similar purpose: to transplant users into a new reality by engaging their senses. What has changed is the technology behind these devices, which allows for an even more immersive experience.

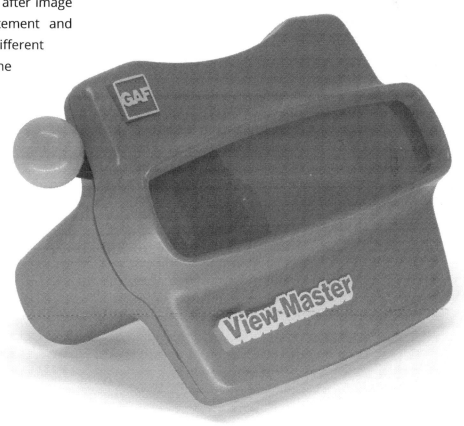

HOW IT WORKS

My old View-Master relied on round paper discs with translucent images lining the circumference of the disc. You slipped a disc into the slot and then looked through the viewer, pointing it toward a light source. In my case, the light source was the sun because I spent most days outside on the front porch. Relying on the stereoscopic principle, each eye saw a slightly different angle of the image. The effect was a three-dimensional scene. And each pull of the lever turned the disc and revealed a new image. *Magic!*

Google Cardboard takes the joy of that simple experience and amplifies it. Rather than a paper disc, Google Cardboard relies on a smartphone. Like the original stereoscopic viewers, the Google Cardboard viewer uses a split-screen format to create photospheres that offer a three-dimensional view of the scene.

For the user, the process is still simple. Install and open the Google Cardboard app on your smartphone, place the phone in the Google Cardboard viewer, and see a whole new world.

Viewing a three-dimensional image is only the beginning. The Google Cardboard app uses the smartphone's accelerometer and allows the user to look around the image. By physically moving your head, you can look in any direction and see the image from a new perspective. For example, if you are watching a video of a skydiver and look up, you will see the parachute. Look down, and you will see the ground coming toward you.

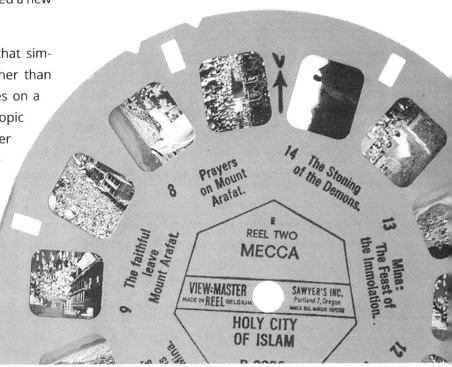

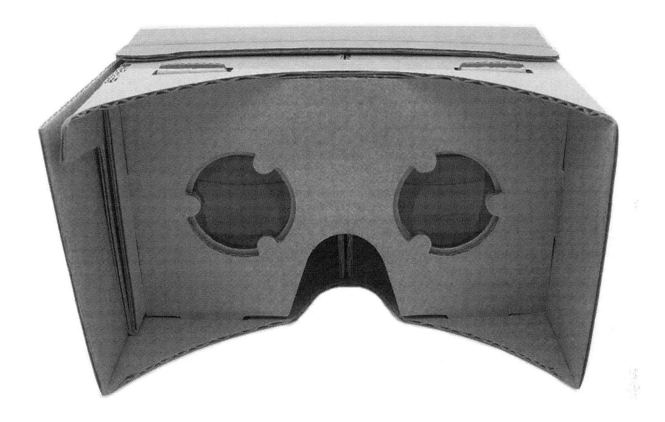

Not every video and photo will work with today's virtual reality (VR) viewers. Special cameras and apps must be used to stitch together multiple images into an equi-rectangular image or video to create a photosphere. Similar to the way a globe is flattened to create a map of the earth, the equi-rectangular image or video is stretched by the app and displayed in a way that allows you to look at the scene from different angles. The effect ends up giving you the view that you might have if you were floating in the center of a glass sphere with an image stretched around the outside of the sphere. You can look up, down, and all around as if you were actually there.

A 20% PROJECT BRINGS EDUCATION TO LIFE

Google Cardboard was born as a 20 percent project. (Google employees are encouraged to spend one day each week, roughly 20 percent of the work week, developing an idea for a new product.) Googlers David Coz and Damian Henry of Paris, France, enthusiastically pitched the idea for a virtual-reality viewer to as many engineers at Google Headquarters in Mountain View, California, as would listen. Eventually, the idea made its way to CEO Larry Page and Vice President of Engineering Sundar Pichai. At Google's 2014 I/O conference a couple months later, Puchai unveiled Google Cardboard V1 by giving every developer in the audience a personal viewer. Since then, developers and producers all over the world have created apps and videos for Google Cardboard and similar virtual-reality headsets. As of December 2016, if you buy a Pixel phone it comes with the latest edition of Cardboard, called Daydream. This viewer comes complete with a remote control and works only with that phone—but more on that later.

It is likely that Google entered the VR world to remain competitive in an emerging market. In doing so, they provided an alternative to similar, but more expensive, technology. As is typical with all Google projects, the company continues to improve upon and add to the cardboard technology, as well as support developers in their efforts to engage consumers interested in the technology. The educational market hasn't been shy in exploring the relatively inexpensive VR headset and accompanying apps. Google responded to educators' interest by making the Google Expeditions app available to teachers. Expeditions is an all-inclusive app that allows teachers to guide and control a classroom full of students using VR headsets on a journey around major landmarks on earth and in space.

FUN FACT

Before creating Google Cardboard, David Coz and Damien Henry worked for the Google Culture Institute, quite possibly one of Google's best-kept secrets. With Google Cardboard, they continue to share the centuries of art and culture with the world.

Google Expeditions
Sylvia Duckworth

Google Expeditions launched in September 2015, and has since been demonstrated in schools around the world with much well-deserved fanfare.

The program allows teachers to take their students on virtual field trips using Google Cardboard and the Google Expeditions apps. Expeditions includes an app for the teacher's tablet and another app for the student device. The great thing about the Expeditions app is that it allows teachers to guide students as they explore.

HOW THE APP WORKS

1. The teacher chooses a destination on the tablet, using the search icon on the top right of the screen.

2. Each destination has multiple views from which to choose.

3. Teachers can see the panorama view, while the students see a smaller area of the image.

4. Teacher controls are extensive, including the ability to see where children are looking (happy face icons), turning on/off ambient sound, opening teacher notes, blacking out students' view, and navigating to the main menu of the destination.

5. Navigations are teacher guided, as the teacher can touch and hold a location to create a focal point for students. Notes about each Expedition destination are provided for the teacher.

6. Happy face icons appear on the teacher's view to show the areas of the image where students are exploring.

TIPS FOR OPERATION

1. Have students sit down on chairs.

2. Review handling guidelines of the equipment.

3. Tell students to "click" for zooming (The zoom feature may not work with all Cardboard viewers.)

4. Rest every few minutes.

5. To have the best viewing experience and keep the device safe inside the viewer, be sure there is no space between the device and viewer. The fit should be snug.

6. Students should place thumbs firmly beneath the viewer, other fingers grasping the top.

7. For the best quality view, make sure that the phone is pushed to the top of the Cardboard and centered.

FINDING GOOGLE EXPEDITION LOCATIONS AND RESOURCES

Map: bit.ly/awesometableGE

Awesome Table:
mrcaffrey.com/google-expeditions-world-map

Andrew Caffrey (@MrCaffrey) has created a map and Awesome Table where you can find exciting destinations to explore.

Complete list of Expeditions (about 100):
bit.ly/TeacherExpeditions

Teacher's Guide:
bit.ly/TeacherExpeditionsGuide

Expeditions Gallery:
bit.ly/ExpeditionsGallery

Teacher-made lessons plans:
bit.ly/GElessonplans

In this book, you will learn how educators are using this simple and exciting technology to help their students explore the world and share their own VR creations. And, you will discover how you can use this tool to make learning fun and interactive—for your students and for you.

Chapter 2
Classroom Uses for Google Cardboard

Donnie Piercey

Field Trips are expensive. And while actually taking students to see new places is definitely the preferred option for exploration, teachers don't always have the financial resources to make that happen. This is one way Google Cardboard can come into play. Using *Google Street View* app (available for iOS and Google Play) or Google Expeditions, your class can take a tour of another city or country.

But taking your students around the world virtually is not the only classroom use for Google Cardboard. You can use this device and its apps to bring many cross-curricular lessons and activities into your lesson plans. Here are a few simple ideas that you can incorporate into your classroom right away.

WRITING

Have your students view a Google Street View image and challenge them to write a story using the image as the setting. If the image includes people, encourage students to incorporate them as characters in their stories.

For elementary-aged students, you can turn the assignment into a sensory writing experience.

After viewing an image, ask students guiding questions such as, "What sounds do you think you'd hear if you were there?" and "What would you smell?" Even better, find a 360º video on YouTube to get the students' creative writing juices flowing!

SCIENCE

Using a Google Cardboard viewer, have students examine 360º images of different habitats from around the world. Then challenge them to identify what types of adaptations animals would need in order to survive in the environment they are viewing.

As students explore photospheres of the planet's polar regions, ask them to look for signs of climate change and/or global warming. Prompt students to develop questions about each photosphere's location and then help them search for the answers.

The Discovery Channel has put together a great VR app for both iOS and Android that hosts hundreds of science-related videos for students to view on Google Cardboard. The videos can serve as springboards for discussion or as supplemental resources for your activities and lessons.

THE ARTS

Using the *Google Art and Culture* (a free app available on both iOS and Android), students can explore art exhibits at more than sixty acclaimed museums around the world with Cardboard. Just imagine! Students will be able to examine entire collections from some of history's most famous artists.

YouTube hosts countless art exhibits and concert videos with 360º views. One of my personal favorites from Carnegie Hall: bit.ly/carnegiehall360.

SOCIAL STUDIES AND HISTORY

After studying various events in history, allow students to use Google Cardboard to take a virtual tour of the locations where the events occurred. Experiencing these historical locations and events will help solidify your students' understanding. After viewing the beaches in Normandy or taking a tour of Independence Hall, for example, your students will have a new appreciation of history.

Example: If your class is studying Islam, head over to the biggest mosque in Africa, located in Casablanca, Morocco. This amazing structure is awe-inspiring and can really capture the grandeur of a well-built mosque. Have students view the different geometric figures and shapes of the mosque. Using Google Street View, students can watch a posted 360º video in their cardboard viewer. They can hear the call to prayer from a Minaret, watch as both men and women begin descending on the mosque in droves, and witness for themselves how each gender goes to a different prayer location. Students can view firsthand the dedication of the Muslims during one of the most sacred pillars of faith, "The Call to Prayer," and get a real-life perspective of what they are learning about history and culture.

LITERATURE

After reading a text or novel, students can view different settings from the story using the Street View app. Or teachers may take the experience a step further and have the students find photospheres connected to the stories themselves as a unique type of formative assessment.

To make it more exciting, teachers can have students share their photos with one another or post them on a blog, directing students to write their own descriptions for the photos that show their understanding of the novel or story.

MATHEMATICS

Put the students in a virtual space and ask them to use non-standard units of measurement to figure out the perimeter, area, or volume of the space (square-foot tiles, etc.).

Using one of the various Roller Coaster apps (available for iOS and Android), have students calculate the height, angles, or velocity at which their cart is traveling.

FIELD TRIP ENHANCEMENT

Prior to taking a field trip, have your students view up-to-date street view images of the destination on Google Cardboard. A virtual preview gives students the opportunity to ask questions like "What's that building over there?" before they even arrive. By previewing and then researching the field trip location, your students will be empowered to ask more informed questions the day of the field trip.

Beyond the Classroom
Lisa Thumann

Google Cardboard and Virtual Reality (VR) aren't just for gaming and virtual field trips. Many industries are currently using and exploring the use of VR. Consider how your students might use this technology in their future careers.

- Welding companies have explored VR as a way to train and interview welders without laying out the high cost of materials and equipment. [1]

- Emergency response teams and law enforcement officials are using VR to prepare themselves for difficult situations. The VR simulations give participants a chance to practice communication, response time, and situational awareness.[2]

- Surgeons and other medical professionals are using VR to simulate surgeries and medical procedures. Using their cellphones and Google Cardboard, the surgeons are able to study specific deformities built off of CT scans.[3]

[1] http://www.thefabricator.com/article/arcwelding/using-virtual-reality-welding-to-evaluate-and-train-welders

[2] http://tucson.com/news/blogs/police-beat/virtual-reality-program-trains-deputies-for-real-cases/article_60f1f953-3ec5-5ed0-9f12-baad70bbf2ab.html

[3] http://www.medgadget.com/2016/01/google-cardboard-virtual-reality-used-prepare-major-pediatric-surgery-video.html

- Some mental health disorders can be treated with VR. Though there is still certainly a place for the intervention of medicine, practitioners can use virtual reality as a tool to administer virtual reality exposure therapy (VRET) for treatment. Through this effective cognitive behavioral therapy, practitioners use VR to expose patients to the triggers for their anxieties and phobias in a controlled environment.[4]

Career training and medical treatments are not the only areas where we are seeing Google Cardboard and virtual reality make in-ways.

 *The New York Times* has released its NYTVR app, which allows the reader to be inside the story.

 Public Speaking for Cardboard allows users to practice speaking in front of a virtual audience.

 Volvo Reality offers the world's first virtual reality test drive.

 VR Accor Hotels for Cardboard offers a virtual tour of this company's hotel chain.

 VR Cinema for Cardboard renders any MP4 video in a split-screen view suitable for playback on virtual reality head-mounted displays, such as Google Cardboard.

---

4 https://techcrunch.com/2016/01/06/virtual-reality-therapy-treating-the-global-mental-health-crisis/

GET CREATIVE!

The magic of Cardboard doesn't have to be exclusive to the classroom. More and more students either have their own devices or can easily get access to one. Encourage your students to start exploring the possibilities of Google Cardboard on their own, and then ask them to share their discoveries with the class.

The concept of virtual reality in the classroom is still in its infancy. What started a few years ago as glorified View-Masters is rapidly transforming into a dynamic tool for classrooms. Likewise, virtual reality content is still relatively new, and there are many apps available in the app store and Google Play that your students can bring into the classroom. Not every app will be suitable for your classroom, but with so many places to explore—both past and present—you'll want to get creative with this learning tool!

8 More Ways to Use VR in the Classroom

1. Trever Reeh (@treverreeh) is a teacher who used the Google Cardboard app for math class, asking students to calculate angles and distances of the Eiffel Tower. Read more: **bit.ly/CardboardMath**

2. Mr. Parkinson (@ICT_MrP) used the Dive City Coaster VR app to inspire creative writing. Read more: **bit.ly/DiveCity**

3. John Zingale (@ihistorywmrjz) and his students used VR for history lessons about Fort Vancouver. Read more: **bit.ly/HistoryVR**

4. Wil Codilla (@WilCodilla) used VR for to take his art students to virtual museums and art galleries. Read more: **bit.ly/ArtClassVR**

5. Richard Bailey (@portodaspartes) is a Spanish teacher who used VR with his students, who described their bedrooms in Spanish. See their project, made with ThingLinkVR: **bit.ly/VRFacebook1**

6. Kim Pollishuke (@KimPollishuke) and Jim Jamieson (@bioloj) are instructional coaches with the York Region District School Board, who created a document with the help of a team of teachers exploring ways to use VR in the classroom. Read more: **bit.ly/vrintheclassroomideas**

7. Try creating a Scavenger Hunt using the Google Street View app and Google Forms. View an example at: **bit.ly/VRForm1**
    Learn how to create a locked form: **bit.ly/lockedformsVR**

8. Have your students create Story Spheres (see Chapter 5). They can create the 360⁰ images themselves or download them from **flickr.com/groups/360degrees/pool**, with the photographers' permission. (You must create a Flickr account to download images, which requires a Yahoo account.)

Chapter 3
Getting Started

Jeffery Heil

Now that you understand what Google Cardboard is and how it could expand learning opportunities in your classroom, it is time to get you set up to use it. This chapter covers the basic equipment you will need: the image device (smartphone or phablet), VR-capable apps or videos, and a VR viewer.

NOTE: Google released Daydream, its new Android VR platform, in the fall of 2016. While this changed some of the hardware and software, the basic VR concept remains the same. Google Cardboard is not going away, as Daydream is only available on Android devices.

THE DEVICE

To experience Google Cardboard, you will need a smartphone or phablet. The two requirements for a device to be VR-headset compatible are that it has a gyroscope and a magnetic field sensor. If you are an iPhone or iPod Touch user, you are all set. If you are an Android user, you can check to see if your device meets the basic requirements by using SensorBox, VR Checker, or EZE VR (apps available in the Google Play Store). The VR headset company FreeflyVR also has a list of compatible devices on its website.[1]

Once you have a VR-ready device, you will want to install a few apps.

---

[1] https://www.freeflyvr.com/compatible/

Thinking About Young Eyes
Lisa Thumann

Most of us remember the concerns that surfaced when the Nintendo 3DS was released in 2011. Countless articles warned that the 3D effects could damage children's eyes if used for extended periods of time. Nintendo ultimately gave in and posted a warning that the 3D devices were not to be used by children younger than six years of age.

Similar concerns have been voiced about VR devices. Some of the more expensive and advanced headsets (like the Gear VR) are not recommended for use by children under the age of thirteen. Even the Nintendo PlayStation 4's VR headset is recommended for children over the age of twelve. However, all of these warnings speak to using these devices for long periods of time, not to using them in an educational setting for forty-five to sixty minutes.

Common sense with these devices in the classroom goes a long way. Limiting viewing to an hour at a time and making sure the student is in a safe location—free from obstacles they might trip over or fall into—are safe practices. Most importantly, if the child is experiencing any type of nausea or disorientation, set the device aside.

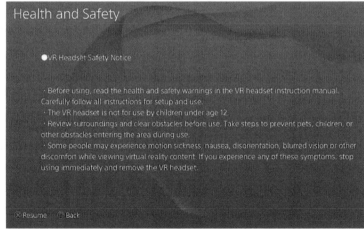

PlayStation VR Headset Warnings

THE APPS

Viewing Apps

The first app to download is the Google Cardboard app itself. It is available for both Android and iOS. You will become very familiar with the Google  Cardboard icon, as it's the icon you will look for as you explore additional apps and tools.

It would be impossible to include a definitive list of Cardboard apps here, as new ones are released almost daily. The best way to stay informed is to find a community of Google Cardboard users and see what apps they are exploring. These communities can be found on Google+, Facebook, Twitter, and through EdTechTeam, among others. Many of EdTechTeam's core members have used and curated content for Google Cardboard since its inception and are happy to share their insights. Two in particular, Jim Sill[2] and Molly Schroeder[3] provide frequently updated lists of resources. Additionally, if you ever get a chance to attend an EdTechTeam Summit, be sure to attend a session on Google Cardboard or VR.

Although countless apps are available for Google Cardboard, there are three apps you may want to start with: Within, Cedar Point, and Google Street View.

Within (formerly called Vrse) claims to offer "extraordinary stories in virtual reality," and it does! Armed with a device and Bluetooth headphones, Within will quickly show you the power of VR. The company produces amazing videos and short films in VR that must be experienced in order to be appreciated.

Cedar Point is one of the better roller coaster VR apps. With it, you will have the experience of being on a roller coaster without leaving the comfort of your home, office, or school.

Google Street View, as you will learn in more detail later in the book, will not only be the starting point for stunning 360° geography in VR, it will also be a place for you to contribute your own 360° images.

One more app to consider as you begin using Google Cardboard is *nytVR*, VR stories created by *The New York Times*. Through nytVR, reporters bring the news to life, allowing users to

---

[2] http://www.mistersill.com/google-cardboard

[3] http://bit.ly/2mecYNg

experience stories from every visual angle. Like Within, nytVR offers a glimpse at the future of VR.

Camera Apps

As you use and become familiar with Google Cardboard, the moment *will* come when you see something and think, *I have to share this!* At that point, you may want to use your device to take some of your own 360º images to view in Cardboard. Here's a brief overview of what you'll need to create your own VR content.

Android Devices

Cameras in Android smartphones and phablets come equipped to take photospheres (360º images). Simply open the camera app, touch the three vertical bars in the upper left of the screen, and choose Photo Sphere. The app will then walk you through the steps of taking your first photosphere.

Cardboard Camera is a separate app that Android users can install to create panoramic images with sound. Cardboard Camera does currently have some limits. The images can only be viewed through the app, and the camera does not take full 360º viewable images;

however, it does nicely blur the top and bottom areas that are not captured to maintain the integrity of the panorama. The addition of audio in the Cardboard Camera app makes the images interesting and unique.

iOS Devices

Cameras on iOS smartphones and phablets do not (as of this writing, anyway) come equipped with the ability to capture 360º images, but there is an app, appropriately named **360 Panorama**, which allows iOS users to take photospheres.

Google Street View Camera App

Google Street View will also allow you to take photospheres with your Android or iOS device's camera. The app works very much like the Android camera's photosphere feature.

As you begin to explore the world of photosphere camera apps, you will likely become hooked on the potential for your own VR content creation. In Chapter 4, you will learn more about other apps and tools you can use to create your own VR content.

Sharing Apps

When you begin to capture your own images, you will want to see and share them. VR technology is constantly changing and improving, but one of my favorite apps for uploading and sharing 360º content is Round.me, available for both iOS and Android.

YouTube also offers the ability to view 360º videos, both with and without a VR viewer. A YouTube channel, 360º Videos, hosts 360º videos. Using a 360° camera like the Ricoh Theta, you can record and host your own immersive videos on your YouTube channel. YouTube's latest feature, immersive video with spatial audio, allows the viewer to experience the potential of 360º video from a PC, YouTube app on Android and iOS, or by using a VR viewer. As you can see, there are many ways to host, view, and share your content, as well as to view the content created and hosted by others.

THE VR VIEWER

Now that you have learned about some of the exciting ways to view VR using your device and apps, it is time to choose a viewer to bring all of this to life. A number of brands and styles of VR viewers are available on the market today (Oculus Rift and Samsung Gear, for example). Because the focus of this book is using Google Cardboard in the classroom, we will discuss viewers created for Google Cardboard. One of the best places to start your search for a viewer is with the Google Cardboard site itself: https://vr.google.com/cardboard/. The site offers suggestions for viewers, apps, developers, and manufacturers. By clicking the *Get Cardboard* link from the menu, you will find more than a dozen suggested viewers, along with instructions on how to "build your own" if you are interested in joining the DIY cardboard movement.

Approximately half with the suggested viewers are constructed of cardboard, the same material used to create the first Google Cardboard viewer. Cardboard viewers are easy to assemble and work well with both iOS and Android smartphones. If you are buying the viewer for personal use, any of the suggested devices will work fine. (Although, if you are feeling nostalgic, you may find that the red Mattel View-Master is just the device to take you back to your childhood.) If you are looking for devices for use in your classroom, especially a classroom of younger kids, you'll want to consider two important factors:

1. *Will it protect the device inside?*
2. *Can it be easily cleaned?*

When considering those two factors, the Mattel View-Master is a personal favorite. It is a solid viewer that can be easily cleaned. Additionally, MAXCases has also produced a cardboard for EdTechTeam (our company, full disclosure), that is made of cardboard, but it is coated with a material that allows the device to be cleaned with an alcohol wipe. They can be ordered direct from MAXCases or purchased at an EdTechTeam Summit. The Google Tech C-1 Glass is compact and includes a carrying case, but it does not hold the device as securely as a teacher may want. If price is an issue, the viewers made of cardboard work wonderfully and can get the classroom teacher much closer to a full set on a limited budget. For additional options, check Amazon.

Regardless of where you shop, be sure to read the reviews and to check that the viewer will fit your device. Some viewers are made for smaller phones, and some are better adapted to the larger phones, or *phablets*, such as the iPhone 6 Plus, the Nexus 6P, and the Samsung Galaxy lines. If you have the opportunity to do so, try out the viewer before you buy—especially if you are purchasing in bulk. Comfort is also something you should consider, especially if the device is something that you will be using frequently.

Now you have enough information to get started with Google Cardboard, but there is no substitute for experience. Get your device ready, download some apps, purchase or make a viewer, and start exploring!

TEACHER TIP

While Google Cardboard viewers are relatively inexpensive ($3–$15), classroom budgets are always tight. Here's an idea to try for the upcoming school year: When putting together your back-to-school supply list, why not make a VR viewer like Google Cardboard a required purchase for students? Even better: Have one of your first in-class activities be for your students to create their own!

See Chapter 6 to learn more about how to make your own Google Cardboard Viewer.

Chapter 4

Creating Content:
Taking 360° Pictures and Videos

Jeffery Heil

Most modern smartphones have the ability to take 360° images. However, capturing an image with a smartphone is neither quick nor easy, and there is currently no app for capturing 360° video on a smartphone. If you really want to begin to create some amazing Google-Cardboard-ready content, both image and video, it is time to level up. We will begin with a new camera.

SPHERICAL CAMERA

We say *spherical camera* instead of 360° camera because many of the consumer-level devices on the market do not produce a full 360° field of view (FOV). This is much like the Google Cardboard Camera that comes as part of the Cardboard app, where the FOV is a full 360° *panorama*, but not a full 360° FOV including every inch and angle of the scene. A few spherical cameras are on the market, but we are going to focus on one in particular: the Ricoh Theta S. Its closest competitor, the Kodak SP360 is a great camera, but to get the full 360° FOV, you will need to use two cameras and the Kodak-provided software to stitch them together. This might be an option for the seasoned enthusiast, but we are going to focus on simplicity in this book.

The Theta S is the latest of the 360° consumer cameras that Ricoh has produced, and it works very well for the average person. It is also the camera most often used by Google enthusiasts. The Theta S costs $349 and is available for purchase online. You can check the camera's Geeky Tech Stats, but it is enough to know that the camera produces high quality images and good video that can be enjoyed with a Google Cardboard viewer. For those looking to save money, the Ricoh Theta m15 will run about $100 less than the Theta S, but you will only have five minutes of consecutive shooting at 15 fps (frames per second) and half of the internal storage. The Ricoh Theta m15 does work very well for images.

Note: Since the initial writing of this chapter, there have been a few newly released cameras into the 360° market. Two of note are the Samsung Gear 360 and the Nikon Key Mission 360. Both shoot 4K video, however, there have been some consumer complaints about stitching the 360° image and the ease of use. The Samsung Gear 360 was created to complement the Samsung Gear VR viewer. One drawback is that, unless you have a Samsung phone and a PC computer, you will find that the camera is not so easy to use. While there are some crafty workarounds, they take away from the ease of use. The Nikon Key Mission 360 will cost almost a third more than the Theta S ($499 versus $350) and its stitching feature has been reported as a big issue; however, it is shockproof and waterproof, which, for some people, may make it worth it to deal with the stitching shortcomings. Even with the new releases, the Theta S is still this author's recommendation.

GEEKY TECH STATS FOR THE THETA S

- Two 12 MP (megapixel) sensors (one on each side) produce a 14 MP image output

- Records HD (high definition) video at 30 fps (frames per second)

- Captures up to 25 minutes of consecutive shooting

- Stores up to 8MB of content

GETTING STARTED WITH YOUR CAMERA

Once you acquire a spherical camera, you will be well equipped to take, host, and share 360° images that can be viewed with Google Cardboard. If you are using the Ricoh Theta S, the first step is to download the Ricoh Theta S app to your device and/or computer (theta360.com/en/support/download/). With the Theta S connected to your computer, you should always check for the latest firmware updates for the camera. One of the most recent firmware updates allowed for the use of a timer on the camera to take still shots. The Theta S app will allow you to transfer images and video to your device that can then be shared on social media, saved to your photos, uploaded to theta360.com, or edited with an Android or iOS app. (You can also find links to helpful apps for editing your 360° images and videos at theta360.com. The Theta+ and Theta+ Video are two of the most popular for editing and sharing content.) In Chapter 5, you'll learn more about sharing your 360° photos and videos with a larger audience.

In order to use the Theta app with your Android or iOS device, you will need to ensure you can connect to the Theta's own Wi-Fi network (usually the name thetaXXX followed by the serial number of the camera). Enable the network by turning on the Wi-Fi button on the side of the camera. Then log on to the network and open the Theta app. There you should find that your device and the theta are connected (or not, in which case you should consult the manual for support). If it is connected, you can control the camera with the app in either photo or video mode. This is very helpful when you do not want your hand and fingers to be a focal point of the image or video, something hard to avoid if you are holding the camera in your hand while shooting. To this end, one piece of helpful equipment to consider buying is a small tripod. We prefer tripods than can double as selfie sticks, like Manfrotto and GorillaPod tripods. The tripods allow you to create some distance from the camera for more interesting shots. When you are selecting a tri-pod, be sure to consider the size of the camera and tripod if you want to carry both to remote areas.

TAKING 360° IMAGES

The art of taking quality 360° images is something that requires time and experience. Think about what you are trying to capture and how you might want to share the image before taking the shot. If you are trying to capture the essence of a location that you would like to eventually view in Google Cardboard, try to get the camera above your head to improve the FOV. Some of the most interesting 360° images obscure the photographer until the person viewing the image looks directly down with the VR viewer. However, there are also times when you want the people, including the photographer, to be part of the subject of the shot. In this case, you would want to experiment with different angles, from low to high, to determine which shots work best for the situation. Whatever the focus of your image, get as close to the subject as possible. Consider that the lenses of most 360° cameras shoot in a type of modified fisheye, so you can get fairly close to the camera without ruining the quality of the shot. Another good idea is to do some research by looking at some of the more interesting VR apps that use images of places and people.

SPHERICAL CAMERAS, 360° IMAGES, AND GOOGLE STREET VIEW

Google Street View is an amazing tool that will allow you to take your students anywhere in the world—in full VR. All Street View images on the app are viewable with Google Cardboard. Of course, one of the easiest ways to get your 360° images ready for viewing in Google Cardboard is to upload and publish them to Google Street View. (**Note**: Be aware that a published Street View image is viewable by anyone with access to Google Maps/Street View.) If you are able to connect your Theta to your device, you can connect the spherical camera (usually the Theta) to Street View. When your smartphone is connected to your camera, and you are logged into the app, any image you take is automatically uploaded to a private area for you to review.

If you like the image, you can publish it to Google Street View. Once you publish your image, you (and others) can view it in Google Cardboard by looking for the Cardboard icon on the image and selecting it. You can also locate your published 360° photos by going to the location where the photo was taken and looking for public photospheres there. Using Google Cardboard and Street View brings an entirely different look and feel to a report on "what I did on my summer vacation."

Most people, when looking at Street View images for the first time in VR, have a visceral reaction to how real the image appears. Think about how this realistic imagery can transform the way we all—teachers and students alike—experience education! Check out the step-by-step instructions on the following pages, created by Sylvia Duckworth, to start using Google Street View with Google Cardboard right away (even if you *don't* have a spherical camera).

How to Create 360° images using the Google Street View App

(Works on All Mobile Devices)

1. Open the Google Street View app.

2. Click on the camera with a plus (+) sign on it.

3. Select one of the following options:

- Spherical camera: If you have a 360° camera like the Ricoh Theta, you can take a photo with it straight from this app.

- Import 360 photos: If you already have a 360 photo on your camera roll, you can upload it to Google Street View here.

- Camera: This is where you tap to take a new 360 photo. Tap on the camera icon to begin capturing the 360° image.

4. Essentially, you are going to stand in one place and turn in a circle, capturing images as you turn. On the screen, you will see the scene in front of you with an orange dot in the middle of the screen. Follow the directions to point your camera/phone at the orange dot until the white circle is centered on the orange dot. As soon as you have the circle and dot aligned, the camera will automatically capture the image. Once the camera takes the first picture, rotate slightly to take the next image. As you move, you will see a new orange dot appear. Align the camera's white circle over the orange dot. The camera will, again, automatically capture the image. Continue to center the white circle on the orange dots. Your device will automatically capture the pictures.

Point the camera at the dot

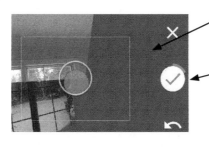

5. Continue turning and aligning the circles and dots until there is no gray area left.

6. Outside the image you're shooting, you will see a white circle with an orange check mark inside it. As you turn and capture images, an orange line will outline the circle to show your progress.

7. When you are done, tap the green checkmark.

8. Next you will see a little man running around putting your photosphere together. When he stops, your photosphere is ready. Tap on it, then tap on the Google Cardboard icon to view it in VR if you have a viewer. (If the screen is just black, hit the back button and try again.)

360° VIDEO

The future of 360° video content is exciting. The present? Well, not so much. Most of today's 360° videos have the quality of poorly shot home videos, but that's okay. We're all still learning! Any new concept or product using a previously unavailable technology goes through an evolution. Much like we discussed in the previous section, some content producers, like Within, nytVR, and Discovery VR are producing exceptional and interesting content. Review it and use those examples to spark your imagination and that of your students. Likewise, YouTube's 360° Video channel hosts a variety of videos. There, you can explore the evolution of 360° content. The rate of improvement—from content that looks homemade to high-quality videos—has been dramatic in the past year alone. And the content quality will only continue to get better. As you create and share your own content, be kind to yourself in the process. Temper your expectations as you learn how to produce better quality videos.

TAKING 360° VIDEO

Much like capturing a quality 360° image, shooting quality 360° videos requires practice. Research others' work to get a feel for the type of video you would like to create, and then experiment with creating your own content.

Even some of the less interesting subjects are made more interesting in VR. If you are using the Ricoh Theta S, you can take up to twenty-five minutes of continuous shooting time. That is a lot of video, although a video of that length is not recommended for social sharing.

When shooting with a Ricoh Theta S or any 360° camera, it is important to have the right tools. Don't forget to use tripods, and even selfie sticks help make the filming of these videos better and more stable. Shooting a 360° video requires a working knowledge of camera techniques and angles, so it might be a good idea to experiment or consult a good YouTube video on creating good video content.

Google Cardboard makes it simple to publish and view your 360° videos. And if you're using the Theta S, your Theta account can be connected to Facebook and Twitter, so you can easily share videos on those platforms. However, the best place to make your video accessible is YouTube. If you are an iPhone user, you can connect your Theta S to your iPhone over Wi-Fi, download the video, and upload it to the YouTube app. For Android users, you can download the video to your computer, convert it using the Theta app (as a file with the .en extension), and then upload to YouTube. Once you upload the video to YouTube as a 360° video, it is easy to view with Google Cardboard—just look for the cardboard icon in the YouTube app on your device, click on it, and watch your video in VR. Plug in headphones for a completely immersive experience.

One of the latest advancements in 360° video is the option to live stream video using a variety of apps. HugVR, YouTube, and Google Hangouts are three places where you can stream a meeting, discussion, or an event. The viewer can even watch the event in Cardboard so they feel like they're part of the action! You will, of course, need to use a 360° camera for this, but it can present a unique way to experience the action.

In the next chapter, you'll learn more about how to share your 360° images and videos in your classroom and with larger audiences.

Chapter 5

Sharing Your Google Cardboard Images and Videos

Sylvia Duckworth

Once you and your students have created 360° content, you need to choose a way to share it. Several options exist for sharing 360° content, and more platforms are becoming available as this form of media gains popularity. In this chapter, you'll learn how to share 360° images and videos.

Some ways to share 360s

1. Google Street View App *

2. Google Maps

3. Google Photos

4. Round.me *

5. Facebook

6. Twitter

7. Google+

8. Story Spheres *

✱ Can view images in VR on a smartphone!

1. Google Street View App

- Open app and tap on "Private" to see your photospheres (you may need to scroll across to the right to see this).

- Scroll down, tap on a 360° image you just took, then tap the three dots and set location. Note that there is an option to blur faces.

You now have the option to share your 360° image privately or publicly.

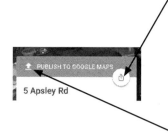

To share **privately**: tap the "Upload" button, then tap "SHARE PRIVATELY." Choose how you want to share. (Note: viewers will not be able to view the image in 360 this way, unless they have an app like Theta S to open it. However, you can share other ways.) Note to Android users: The 360 will save automatically on your camera roll. Note to iOS users: Tap on "Save image" to save on your camera roll.

To share **publicly**: tap on the photosphere, then "Publish to Google Maps." Tap "Publish" again. Tap on the back button, and then tap on "Profile." Your photosphere should show here. (Note: It's a bit glitchy and may not show right away.)

Now you can share your 360° image on social media.

1. From the app, tap "Profile."

2. Select a 360° image from the list. (Note: You can link photospheres together. Tap two 360s and then tap "Connect 360 Photos." Try it out—super cool!)

3. Tap the "Share" icon.

4. You can share in a number of different ways. Note that the link you send will direct the viewer to Google Maps.

2. Google Maps

1. If you published your 360° video in the Google Street View app, it means that it will now appear in Google.com/maps on your desktop.

2. Tap the "Menu" icon (the three bars in the top left-hand corner) and scroll down to "Your Contributions."

3. Tap "Photos." Scroll down and tap on the photosphere you want to share.

4. Copy the URL to share.

Notes: As of the printing of this book, viewers *cannot* view photospheres in Virtual Reality from Google maps (only from the Google Street View app).

3. Google Photos

- You need to download Google Photos to your desktop and mobile device before sharing this way. Download/install the Google Photos app for your desktop and iOS or Android device.

- If you already sync your phone photos to Google Photos, you can go to Photos.Google. com on your desktop and share from there. Simply tap the photo, then the share icon to see what platform options are available for sharing. (Note: Syncing is much faster from an Android phone than from an iPhone. Be patient.)

- Google's support page offers help for learning how to sync your photos to Google Photos (https://support.google.com/photos/.) Note: If this is the first time to sync your photos, it might take a long for them to upload.

Notes

- If you have an Android phone, you can share directly from the Photos app on your phone to Facebook. (The image will be flat if you share to other platforms.) Tap on the photo, then tap the share icon.

- Viewers *cannot* view photospheres in Virtual Reality from Google Photos.

4, 5, 6, 7: Round.me, Facebook, Twitter, and Google+

In my opinion, the Round.me website and app is the best way to share photospheres. Once an image is uploaded, you can share on many different platforms. You can also share the URL and people can view your 360s in VR. You need to create an account, which can be done from the website or from the app. (Users need to be 13+ years old, so consider creating a class account for students. You can see my class account here: https://roundme.com/@lscrescent.) The poster below hangs in my classroom to remind students how to access the account. The only drawback to Round.me is that it limits free accounts to a maximum of fifteen uploads per week. After that, you need to buy a pro account. Here's how to use Round.me to distribute your images on a variety of social media platforms:

1. Go to the Round.Me website on your mobile device (iOS: use Safari; Android: use Chrome).

2. Tap on the three bars in the top right corner.

3. Sign up or log in. (You may have to tap on the three bars again after logging in.)

4. Tap "Create space."

Round.me

To upload: **sduckworth@crescentschool.org**
password: cslsg326

To visit: **round.me/@lscrescent**

5. Tap on the blue word "Browse."

6. Scroll for your 360 (for iOS, go to Photo Library> Camera Roll > Tap Photo > Done. For Android, go to Documents > Images > Panoramas > Tap Photo). Note: If you can't find your 360 and you created it with the Google Street View app, go back to the app and email it to yourself from the app. Save the 360 on your desktop then upload to Round.me from your desktop.

7. Upload your 360.

8. Give your 360 a title.

9. Turn "Published" on, then click "Save."

10. To share your 360, open the Round.me app.

11. Tap the three bars.

12. Tap your name.

13. Tap your 360, then the "Share" button.

14. Now you can share in many different ways, and the image will always be in 360 mode.

To view a 360 in VR, turn your device sideways and tap the Cardboard icon (iOS). For Android, tap the three bars then the Cardboard icon.

Notes:

- You can also get an embed code for your 360 from the desktop Round.me site by clicking on the three dots > Published > double click on image > three dots > share and embed.

- To create hot spots on your 360 images from your desktop, tap the "eye," then tap "i."

8. Sharing with Story Spheres

Storyspheres.com by Google, in Beta, is used to create narrated stories with 360° images (must use with Chrome). Visit the link that follows for an example: bit.ly/storysphere. Here's how to use Story Spheres to share your 360° images:

1. Open your mobile device camera roll and find your 360 image. Email the 360 to yourself. If you can't find your 360 and you made it with the Google Street View app, open the app and email it to yourself from there.

2. On your laptop, save the image to your desktop.

3. Create an audio track to go with your image. Use a voice recorder, either on your laptop or on your mobile device (it has to be .mp3). Save audio file to your desktop. You can also upload a music background.

4. Go to Storyspheres.com and sign in with your Google account.

5. Tap the three bars on top left hand corner, then tap "Create."

6. Title your image and agree to terms, then tap "Create."

7. Tap "Upload Files" and upload your 360° image and audio tracks either individually or at the same time. If you are uploading a speaking audio track and a music track, you can adjust the volumes later (see 11 below).

8. Tap "Next."

> ### GET YOUR FREE MUSIC HERE!
>
> Jamendo.com
>
> FreePlayMusic.com
>
> Incompetech.com
>
> BenSound.com
>
> Purple-Planet.com
>
> YouTube .com/audiolibrary/music
>
> Dig.CCmixer.org
>
> AudioNautix.com

9. Wait until the project loads, then tap "Preview."

10. Tap X, then three bars, then "My Story Spheres" to find the image again.

11. Tap "Studio" or "Next" to edit. You will see these controls (below). Play with them to see how they affect the audio volume as you scroll around the image. These controls are important if you have more than one audio file embedded in your image. Mike Downes provides a detailed video tutorial with more information on how to add hotspots to your 360 here: bit.ly/howtostorysphere.

12. When you are happy with your Story Sphere, tap "Save." Tap "Share" to share on different social media (tap the icons), or just "View" and copy the URL to share with others.

> **NOTE**
>
> Story Spheres can be seen in VR!

HOW TO SHARE 360° VIDEOS

At the moment, the only way to take good quality 360° videos is with a 360° camera. As discussed in the previous chapter, the Ricoh Theta is an excellent, easy-to-use option.

The easiest way to upload 360° videos to YouTube is to transfer your video from the 360° camera to the camera roll of your iOS mobile device, then open the YouTube app and tap the camera icon.

Since it is not possible to upload to YouTube wirelessly from an Android device, you have a couple of options. The easiest is to transfer the video from the 360° camera to the iPad wirelessly, then upload to YouTube from the iPad. If you don't have an iOS device, you will need to transfer the video from the 360° camera to your desktop; however, it gets complicated because the video will not be in the right format to upload. Learn more with this tutorial here: bit.ly/SylTheta.

HOW TO LIVESTREAM 360° VIDEO

It is possible to live stream video from a 360° camera like the Ricoh Theta. The easiest way is to use the website: HugVR.com.

1. Sign up for an account with HugVR.com.

2. Download the Theta UVC Blender at theta360.com and use it to convert the dual fisheye view to a rectangular view. It will ask you to connect your camera (turned off) to register it.

3. Put your camera in Live mode by holding the top and bottom buttons at the same time. Note that you will need a special extension for your tripod to do this.

4. Plug your camera in to your laptop, using the USB cord.

5. In HugVR, click on "Go Live."

6. All live streams are archived so they can be viewed later.

It is possible to livestream 360° video via YouTube, but it is extremely complicated. Visit bit.ly/LiveStream360 to learn how.

> ## NOTE
>
> HugVR isn't flawless. Sometimes it works; sometimes it doesn't. One tip from the developer is to use it with the Firefox browser.

Chapter 6
Make Your Own Google Cardboard Viewer

Donnie Piercey

While there are many sites available for teachers and students to bulk purchase class sets of Google Cardboard (imcardboard.com, for example), why not have students create their own instead? By creating their own VR headsets, students will be able to take ownership in their learning right from the start of the school year. Google Cardboard viewers also make for great Makerspace projects.

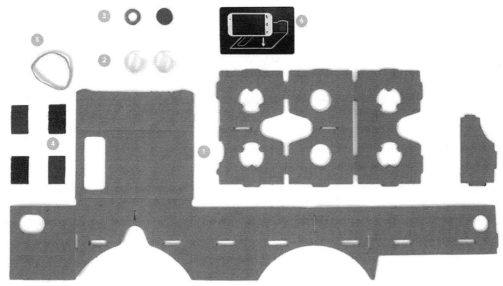

Image credit: https://vr.google.com/cardboard/get-cardboard/

Acquiring the pieces you need requires some setup and planning. You can find kits available online (they run about $10.00), where the supplies needed to create cardboard can be purchased. In a nutshell, students can tape the template onto the piece of cardboard and then cut out their soon-to-be Google Cardboards. If you teach younger students, this is where a teacher's aide or a helpful parent volunteer will come in handy.

However, simply cutting out a template doesn't allow your phone to turn into a 360⁰ viewer. To create your own, you will need to purchase a few other things as well:

- 2 bi-convex lenses (25mm, focal length 45mm). You should be able to find a pair for between $3 and $5 on Amazon.

- Strips of Velcro®. These are used to hold the viewer shut once your phone is inside.

- 1 ¾-inch neodymium magnet, easily found at a craft store

- 1 ¾-inch ceramic magnet

- Rubber band

Altogether, the cost for these additional materials should be about $10.00. Sites like Amazon.com or other third-party sellers usually package all of these pieces together. It is important to note that these parts are needed to create Cardboard 1.0. The 2.0 version doesn't require the magnets to function; it uses conductive tape to simulate a finger tapping on an iPhone or Android screen. The 2.0 version is a bit more difficult to create.

Once you have the parts you need, you can begin to create the viewers themselves.

Several templates are available online. One example can be found here: bit.ly/cardboardtemplate. These templates can be printed out and then taped onto whatever sheet of cardboard you're going to create the viewer from. Choosing the right cardboard material is important. If the piece of cardboard you are creating from is too thick, your students won't be able to cut or fold it as easily. While thinner cardboard is easier to slice, cut, and fold, it'll be much more susceptible to tearing and won't hold up to regular classroom use over the course of the year.

Once cut out, your Google Cardboard is almost ready! The final step in creating your own Google Cardboard can be the trickiest. The viewer will need to be folded in on itself, taped together, and affixed with the Velcro.

Speaking from experience, my school district's (Eminence Schools) first foray into cutting out and folding cardboard by hand didn't end up anything close to perfect. (See figure 6.1)

Figure 6.1

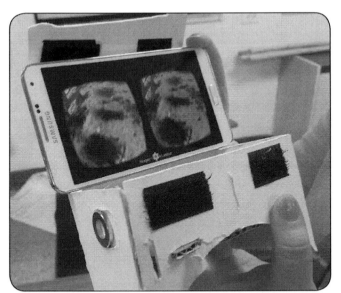

Figure 6.2

Later versions created by our students had a much cleaner look to them. You can see that we upgraded the material and switched to using craft knives rather than scissors for a cleaner cut. (See figure 6.2)

If your district has a makerspace with a laser cutter, try using it to cut out your Cardboard viewers. (See figure 6.3) Here is a link to the Corel Draw file via Makerspath. com that you can use on your laser cutter: bit.ly/coreldrawcardboard.

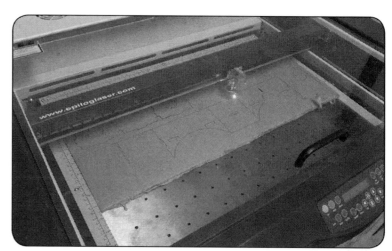

figure 6.3

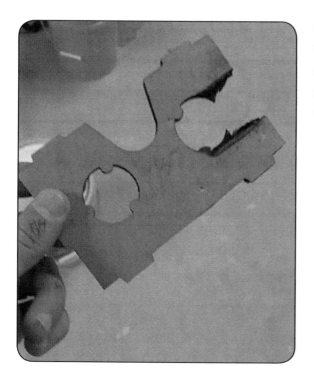

Caution: Do not walk away from your Google Cardboard while it is being cut out on the laser cutter. Depending on the type of cardboard used and the strength of your laser cutter, there is a small risk of fire.

I learned this firsthand last year.

The nice part about using a laser cutter, as opposed to cutting out your design with a craft knife, is the finished product. The laser cutter provides a much more professional look.

Chapter 7
Additional Apps and Resources

As VR gains popularity, developers are creating more and more apps to capitalize on consumer interest. Any search for VR in the iOS App store or in the Google Play store will turn up hundreds of apps free and for sale, many of which have questionable educational value. In addition, VR apps also take up tons of storage space on a mobile device, and they are real battery drainers. So how does a teacher distinguish the must-have apps from the chaff?

Largely, by word of mouth. Start asking educators who use VR about the apps they prefer. They will likely have quite a few recommendations for you.

On the next page, we've listed a few sites and apps you may want to check out. Some were mentioned in previous chapters but have been included here for easy reference.

Google Cardboard Official Site
vr.google.com/cardboard

Google Expeditions
google.com/edu/expeditions

Google Cultural Institute
google.com/culturalinstitute

Google Art Project
google.com/culturalinstitute/about/artproject

Google Street View

Within (previously Vrse)
with.in

Discovery Channel's DiscoveryVR
discoveryvr.com

Cedar Point VR App
Available on Google Play and iTunes App store

nytVR
bit.ly/NYTExample

Volvo Reality
bit.ly/VolvoExample

VR Cinema for Cardboard
bit.ly/CinemaExample

Public Speaking for Cardboard
bit.ly/CinemaExample

VR AccorHotels
bit.ly/AccorHotelsExample

JauntVR.com
bit.ly/JauntExample

Jaime Donnally's (@jamiedonnally) collection of VR apps for education
bit.ly/JDExample

YouTube 360⁰ Videos
bit.ly/YouTubeExample

For other great 360° YouTube channels search for the following:

- Discovery 360 YouTube videos

- Google Spotlight Stories

- 360 Labs YouTube videos

- Trending YT 360 videos

Now What?

Holly Clark

While Google Cardboard and Expeditions are new and exciting, they truly are more than a shiny new object. Once you witness the excitement on the faces of students and adults alike, you know there is something real and valuable here—and this benefit applies to education as well.

Remember learning about coral reefs as a child, seeing the pictures, and then trying to imagine what they might be like in real life? This experience is now very different for students. Now students can grab a cardboard or viewer and virtually dive into the ocean, watch the fish feed off the reefs, and easily observe just how many fish make up a school—all while being virtually underwater. Students can get up close and personal at the Burj Khalifa, the world's tallest building in Dubai, visit the pyramids, and even virtually walk down the halls of the Sistine Chapel, painted over five centuries ago.

While being transported to amazing and far-away places is the wow factor that captures students' attention, VR is not all about traveling somewhere or seeing something for the first time. What Google Cardboard viewers create is the opportunity for students to become creators—creators of content and information they can share with the world. What about a school tour that is the highlight of the school website created by fourth graders? That is the kind of content that says *we are getting kids at this school ready for their future*. The virtual tour would be a 360° video directed, scripted, and produced by students. This type of assignment is authentic and provides students with a real audience. They could show their digital and informational savviness by crafting a piece that explains and highlights all the notable parts of their school and the innovative learning that is happening there.

Virtual reality is also about capturing those typical school moments in a new and exciting way. Can you imagine a 360º video creation of a graduation ceremony or school play? Imagine sharing the geographical features of your city with a school in another part of the world, along with videos and explanations created by kids for kids. Here in San Diego, we live near the Pacific Ocean. Imagine the educational images we could share and narrate—all as an assignment.

If the saying holds true that video is the new content, then 360º videos are the new experience.

UP NEXT: DAYDREAM AND VR EXPERIENCES

It was 2014 when Google announced Cardboard, and we were not sure what to do with it until Expeditions was announced. Teachers everywhere cheered. Many teachers even found themselves stalking Google's Expeditions website to find out how they could get Expeditions to their schools. Companies like Best Buy are now selling Google Expeditions Kits, making it even easier to take students on these virtual reality field trips—200 or more of them—without leaving the classroom.

Fast-forward three years later, and Google's latest creation—or VR viewer, Daydream— is a cross between Cardboard and Wii. Although it looks and feels like a breathable, fabric-softened Cardboard device, I noticed a difference as soon as I picked up the remote. The experience seemed a bit more immersive because I had a controller in my hand that allowed me to point at movies I want to watch, 360º video trips I want to explore, or even become part of a gaming experience. Google's Daydream is just the next step in what is sure to become hardware that is part of every household and classroom within the next decade.

With Daydream, even if you just simply want to watch a video, there is a theater-like experience that is a fun twist on watching YouTube videos or even Netflix content.

Beyond even the scope of Daydream is a company out of Melbourne, Australia, that is involved in creating VR content that would allow textbooks to come to life. Imagine hovering over some battle or historical event and watching as the content comes to life. As a student, you would witness the event as it unfolds and maybe even hear reenactments from actors—all from your viewer. We are not sure what this will look like once finished, but it is great that companies are coming up with ways to help us all rethink the educational experience.

VR content and viewers are going to be changing—and changing fast. So get in the know, and share what you have learned with other educators. Together, we can engage and inspire students in a way most of us never dreamed possible.

Stay Connected with EdTechTeam Press!

Get free ebooks and updates at **bit.ly/Press17**.

Want to order an EdTechTeam edition Maxcases cardboard
for yourself or order in bulk for your class?
Just visit **edtechteam.press**.

Once you get the cardboard viewer, visit **bit.ly/ETTCardboard**
to watch a YouTube tutorial by Jim Sill to learn how to put it together.

More Books from EdTechTeam Press
edtechteam.com/books

The HyperDoc Handbook
Digital Lesson Design Using Google Apps

By Lisa Highfill, Kelly Hilton, and Sarah Landis

The HyperDoc Handbook is a practical reference guide for all K–12 educators who want to transform their teaching into blended-learning environments. *The HyperDoc Handbook* is a bestselling book that strikes the perfect balance between pedagogy and how-to tips while also providing ready-to-use lesson plans to get you started with HyperDocs right away.

Assessment That Matters
Using Technology to Personalize Learning

By Kim Meldrum

In *Assessment That Matters*, Kim Meldrum explains the three types of assessment— assessment *as* learning, assessment *for* learning, and assessment *of* learning. Within her instruction on gathering rich assessment information, you'll find simple strategies and tips for using today's technology to allow students to demonstrate learning in creative and innovative ways.

Innovate with iPad
Lessons to Transform Learning in the Classroom

By Karen Lirenman and Kristen Wideen

Written by two primary teachers, this book provides a complete selection of clearly explained, engaging, open-ended lessons to change the way you use iPad in the classroom. It features downloadable task cards, student-created examples, and extension ideas to use with your students. Whether you have access to one iPad for your entire class or one for each student, these lessons will help you transform learning in your classroom.

The Space
A Guide for Educators

By Rebecca Louise Hare and Robert Dillon

The Space supports the conversation around revolution happening in education today concerning the reshaping of school spaces. This book goes well beyond the ideas for learning-space design that focuses on Pinterest-perfect classrooms and instead discusses real and practical ways to design learning spaces that support and drive learning.

A Learner's Paradise
How New Zealand Is Reimagining Education

By Richard Wells

What if teachers were truly trusted to run education? In *A Learner's Paradise*, Richard Wells outlines New Zealand's forward-thinking education system in which teachers are empowered to do exactly that. With no prescribed curriculum, teachers and students work together to create individualized learning plans—all the way through the high school level. From this guidebook, you'll learn how New Zealand is reimagining education and setting an example for innovative educators, parents, and school districts to follow.

Classroom Management in the Digital Age
Effective Practices for Technology-Rich Learning Spaces

By Heather Dowd and Patrick Green

Classroom Management in the Digital Age helps guide and support teachers through the new landscape of device-rich classrooms. It provides practical strategies to novice and expert educators alike who want to maximize learning and minimize distraction. Learn how to keep up with the times while limiting time wasters and senseless screen-staring time.

The Google Apps Guidebook
Lessons, Activities, and Projects Created by Students for Teachers

By Kern Kelley and the Tech Sherpas

The Google Apps Guidebook is filled with great ideas for the classroom from the voice of the students themselves. Each chapter introduces an engaging project that teaches students (and teachers) how to use one of Google's powerful tools. Projects are differentiated for a variety of age ranges and can be adapted for most content areas.

Dive into Inquiry
Amplify Learning and Empower Student Voice

By Trevor MacKenzie

Dive into Inquiry beautifully marries the voice and choice of inquiry with the structure and support required to optimize learning. With *Dive into Inquiry* you'll gain an understanding of how to best support your learners as they shift from a traditional learning model into the inquiry classroom where student agency is fostered and celebrated each and every day.

If I Were a Wizard
By Paul Hamilton

Currently, there is a global push for coding in education. Coding is the new creation tool and it gives us the ability to design new products, bring people together, and solve important problems in the world. Our youngest students learn concepts in many different ways and look for ways to connect concepts to their own lives. *If I Were a Wizard* by Paul Hamilton is designed to bridge the gap between the physical and digital and be a springboard into the magical world of coding.

Code in Every Class
How All Educators Can Teach Programming

By Kevin Brookhouser, M.Ed. and Ria Megnin

In Code in Every Class, Kevin Brookhouser and Ria Megnin explain why computer science is critical to your students' future success. With lesson ideas and step-by-step instruction, they show you how to take tech education into your own hands and open a world of opportunities to your students. And here's the best news: You *don't* have to be a computer genius to teach the basics of coding.

Sketchnotes for Educators
100 Inspiring Illustrations for Lifelong Learners

By Sylvia Duckworth

Sketchnotes for Educators contains 100 of Sylvia Duckworth's most popular sketchnotes, with links to the original downloads that can be used in class or shared with colleagues. Interspersed throughout the book are reflections from Sylvia about what motivated her to create the drawings as well as commentary from many of the educators whose work inspired her sketchnotes.

Making Your School Something Special
Enhance Learning, Build Confidence, and Foster Success at Every Level

By Rushton Hurley

In *Making Your School Something Special*, educator and international speaker Rushton Hurley explores the mindsets, activities, and technology that make for great learning. You'll learn how to create strong learning activities and make your school a place where students and teachers alike want to be—because it's where they feel energized, inspired and *special.*

About the Authors

Holly Clark

Holly Clark is an award-winning educator based in San Diego, California. She is both a National Board Certified Teacher and Google Certified Innovator. Holly has been using Expeditions in the classroom since 2016, and loves using her Ricoh Theta to capture 360° photos and videos when she travels. Holly holds an MA in Technology and Education from Columbia University, New York.

Favorite use of Cardboard

Taking it to a dinner party instead of wine and letting people experience VR as a fun after-dinner activity.

Sylvia Duckworth

Sylvia Duckworth teaches French and technology at Crescent School in Toronto, Canada. She is a Google Certified Innovator and Trainer. She and her grade 3–6 students love creating their own VR content with the Google Street View app on their iPads.

Favorite use of Cardboard

Putting on a rollercoaster app on and trying it out on people.

Jeffery Heil

Jeffery Heil is a Digital Learning Innovator with the San Diego County Office of Education. He has spent more than twenty years working with at-risk, incarcerated, and homeless youth. As a Google Certified Innovator, Educator, and Trainer, he believes technology is the perfect tool to give a voice to the voiceless, whether it be film, photography, art, music, or writing. He is addicted to taking photos with his Google Pixel, capturing the world in 360°, and sharing images to Google Maps and Street View.

Favorite use of Cardboard

Taking people to places they have never been in full virtual reality.

David Hotler

David Hotler is an advocate for the productive use of technology in all subject areas of education and is currently teaching English in Madrid, Spain. He is a Google Certified Innovator and Trainer and is also an avid producer (and consumer) of VR content for Cardboard and YouTube.

Favorite use of Cardboard

Downloading a video on the app Within, putting on some big over-ear headphones, and getting lost in some faraway place.

Donnie Piercey

Donnie Piercey is a fifth grade teacher and technology integration specialist in Eminence, Kentucky. He's spent the past eleven years working as a classroom teacher and loves taking his students to places they've never been, especially with Cardboard. They've worked together to map and share their community's story using 360° imagery and virtual reality.

Favorite use of Cardboard

Watching others watch 360° videos on Cardboard.

Lisa Thumann

Lisa, a former classroom teacher, oversees EdTechTeam's professional development offerings in the United States and works with districts and organizations to customize workshops and events. Lisa is a Google Innovator and a Google Certified Trainer. She presents at national conferences, workshops and in classrooms on how to integrate G Suite and other emerging and engaging technologies into the classroom. Lisa holds a Masters of Arts in Teaching.

Favorite use of Cardboard

That moment when you hand Google Cardboard over to a teacher and they are able to walk up the The Palace of Versailles.

50099182R00038

Made in the USA
San Bernardino, CA
13 June 2017